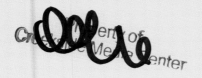

A WEEK

by Robin Nelson

first step nonfiction

Lerner Publications Company · Minneapolis

A **calendar** keeps track of
days, weeks, and **months.**

S	M	T	W	TH	F	S

January
		1	2	3	4	5
6	7	8	9	10	11	12
13	14	15	16	17	18	19
20	21	22	23	24	25	26
27	28	29	30	31		

February
					1	2
3	4	5	6	7	8	9
10	11	12	13	14	15	16
17	18	19	20	21	22	23
24	25	26	27	28		

March
					1	2
3	4	5	6	7	8	9
10	11	12	13	14	15	16
17	18	19	20	21	22	23
$^{24}/_{31}$	25	26	27	28	29	30

April
	1	2	3	4	5	6
7	8	9	10	11	12	13
14	15	16	17	18	19	20
21	22	23	24	25	26	27
28	29	30				

May
			1	2	3	4
5	6	7	8	9	10	11
12	13	14	15	16	17	18
19	20	21	22	23	24	25
26	27	28	29	30	31	

June
						1
2	3	4	5	6	7	8
9	10	11	12	13	14	15
16	17	18	19	20	21	22
$^{23}/_{30}$	24	25	26	27	28	29

July
	1	2	3	4	5	6
7	8	9	10	11	12	13
14	15	16	17	18	19	20
21	22	23	24	25	26	27
28	29	30	31			

August
				1	2	3
4	5	6	7	8	9	10
11	12	13	14	15	16	17
18	19	20	21	22	23	24
25	26	27	28	29	30	31

September
1	2	3	4	5	6	7
8	9	10	11	12	13	14
15	16	17	18	19	20	21
22	23	24	25	26	27	28
29	30					

October
	1	2	3	4	5	
6	7	8	9	10	11	12
13	14	15	16	17	18	19
20	21	22	23	24	25	26
27	28	29	30	31		

November
					1	2
3	4	5	6	7	8	9
10	11	12	13	14	15	16
17	18	19	20	21	22	23
24	25	26	27	28	29	30

December
1	2	3	4	5	6	7
8	9	10	11	12	13	14
15	16	17	18	19	20	21
22	23	24	25	26	27	28
29	30	31				

There are 52 weeks in a **year.**

There are about 4 weeks in
a month.

There are 7 days in a week.

Weeks help us plan what
we are going to do.

I write what I do on
a calendar.

Monday begins the school week.

Tuesday I play baseball.

Wednesday I play piano.

Thursday I help fold clothes.

Friday I watch a movie.

We call Saturday and
Sunday the weekend.

On the weekend, we don't
go to school.

On the weekend, we spend
time with our families.

Then we start a new week.

What do you do each day
of the week?

How much time do you spend doing homework each week?

You can make a line graph to show how much time you spend doing something each week. Look at the line graph at the right to find out which day this child had the most homework. Which days had the least amount of homework? Which days had the same amount of homework?

Minutes Spent on Homework This Week

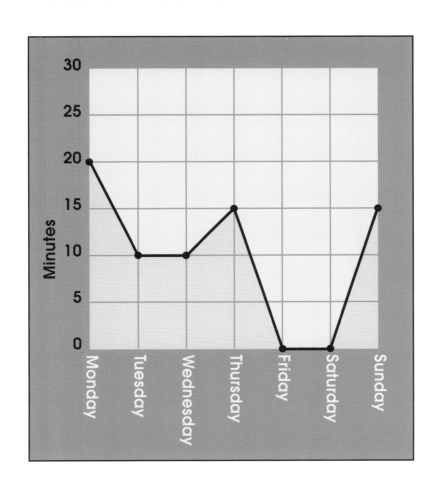

Fun Week Facts

 It takes one week to make jelly beans.

 A shark can grow a new set of teeth in a week.

 The average U.S. household serves chicken at home between two and three times per week.

 Saturday night is the most popular night of the week for eating pizza in America.

A housefly lives a little more than a week.

 An ant can survive for up to two weeks underwater.

 Roaches can live without food for a month, but will only survive a week without water.

 The average child watches about 18 hours of TV a week.

Glossary

 calendar – keeps track of days, weeks, and months

 day – the time from one morning to the next morning. A day is 24 hours.

 month – a part of the year. There are 12 months in a year.

 week – an amount of time. There are 7 days in a week.

 year – an amount of time. There are 12 months in a year.

Index

The photographs in this book are reproduced through the courtesy of: © Todd Strand/Independent Picture Service, front cover, pp. 2, 4, 5, 6, 7, 13, 22 (all); © Trip/S. Grant, p. 8; © E.M. Johansson/Photo Network, p. 9; © Myrleen Cate/Photo Network, p. 10; © Laura Martin/Visuals Unlimited, p. 11; © Stockbyte, p. 12; © Phyllis Picardi/Photo Network, p. 14; © Esbin-Anderson/Photo Network, p. 15; © Trip/T. Freeman, p. 16; © Chad Ehlers/Photo Network, p. 17.

Lerner Publications Company
A division of Lerner Publishing Group
241 First Avenue North
Minneapolis, MN 55401 U.S.A.

Website address: www.lernerbooks.com

Library of Congress Cataloging-in-Publication Data

Nelson, Robin, 1971–
     A week / by Robin Nelson.
          p.   cm. — (First step nonfiction)
     Includes index.
     Summary: An introduction to calendars and the days of the week.
     ISBN: 0–8225–0178–3 (lib. bdg. : alk. paper)
     1. Calendar—Juvenile literature. 2. Week—Juvenile literature. [1. Calendar. 2. Week.
3. Days.] I. Title. II. Series.
CE85.N45 2002
529'.2—dc21   2001002205

Manufactured in the United States of America
1 2 3 4 5 6 – AM – 07 06 05 04 03 02